Color Now, Crochet Later is a Yarn Themed Coloring Book
designed and illustrated by Brianna Iaropoli of Life and Yarn, a Modern Crochet Designer.

Inspired by her own crochet patterns, *Color Now, Crochet Later* features beautiful fiber
related artwork, florals and abstract coloring pages for any coloring enthusiast to enjoy!

Free Drawn Coloring Pages have been organically created, while Project Based Coloring Pages
have been created from crochet patterns you can actually make!

Scan the QR Code below for more information and an index of which pages reference
Life and Yarn's Crochet Patterns by Brianna Iaropoli so that you may
Color Now and Crochet Later!

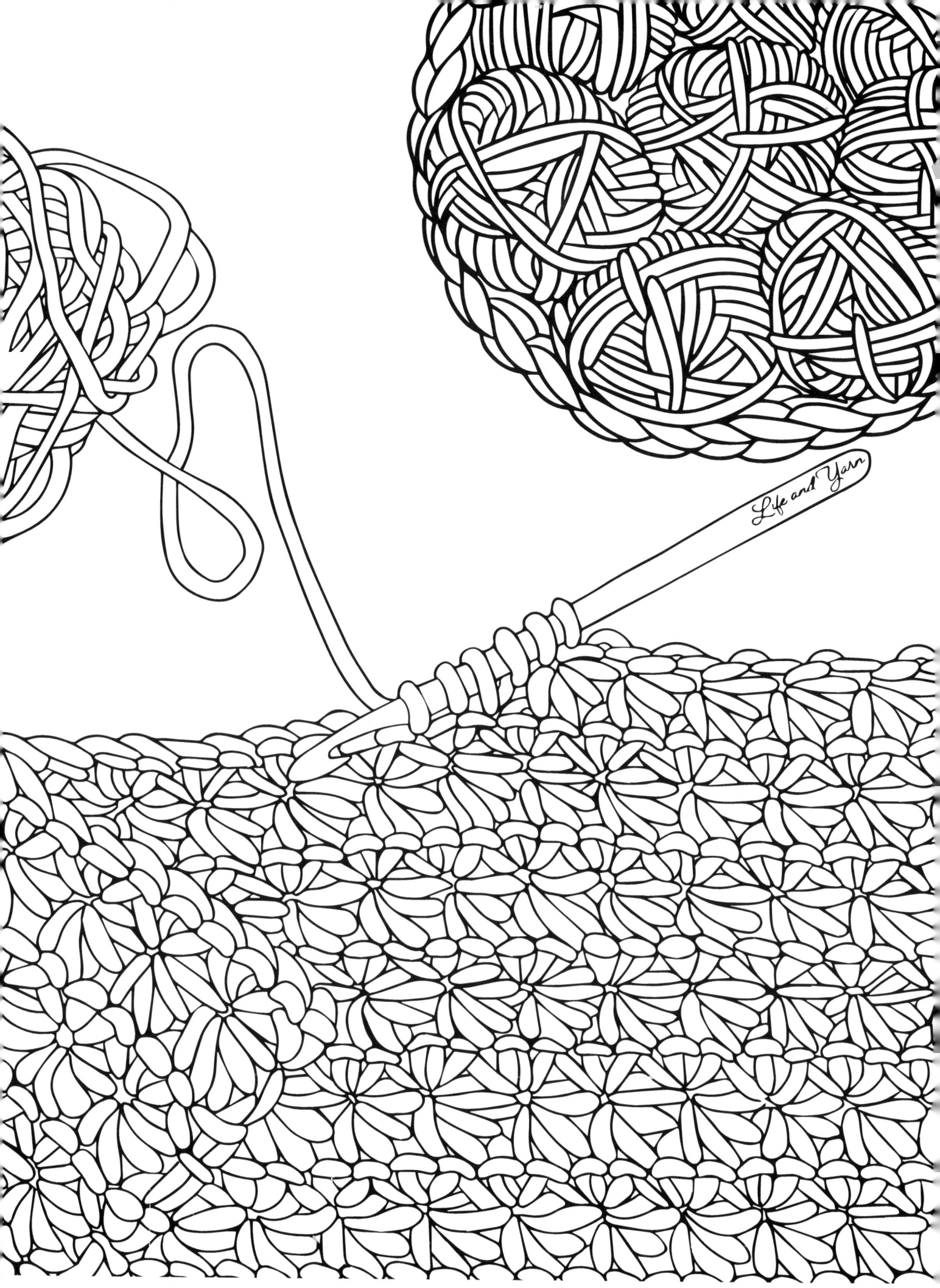

I like big...

HOOKS

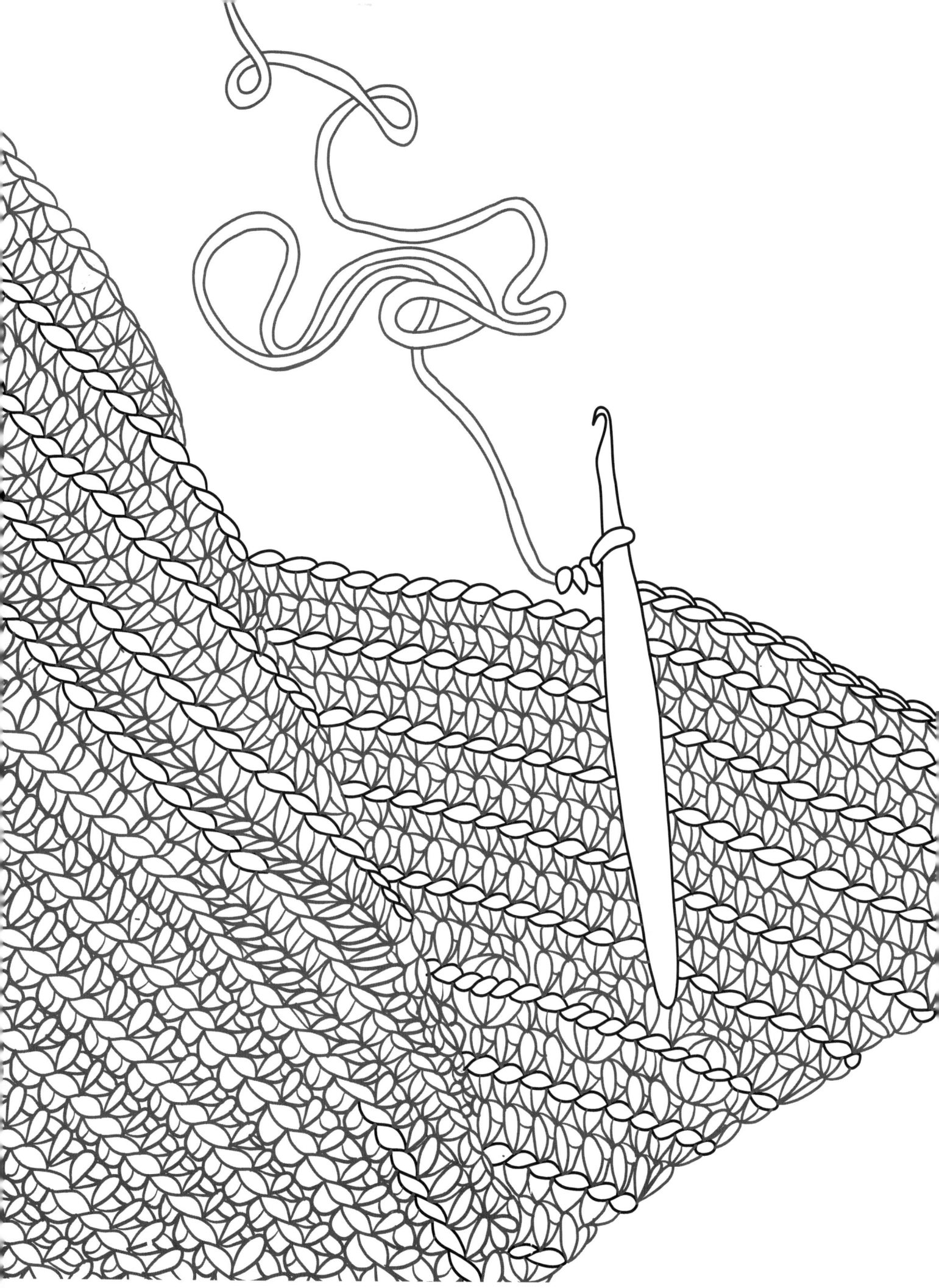

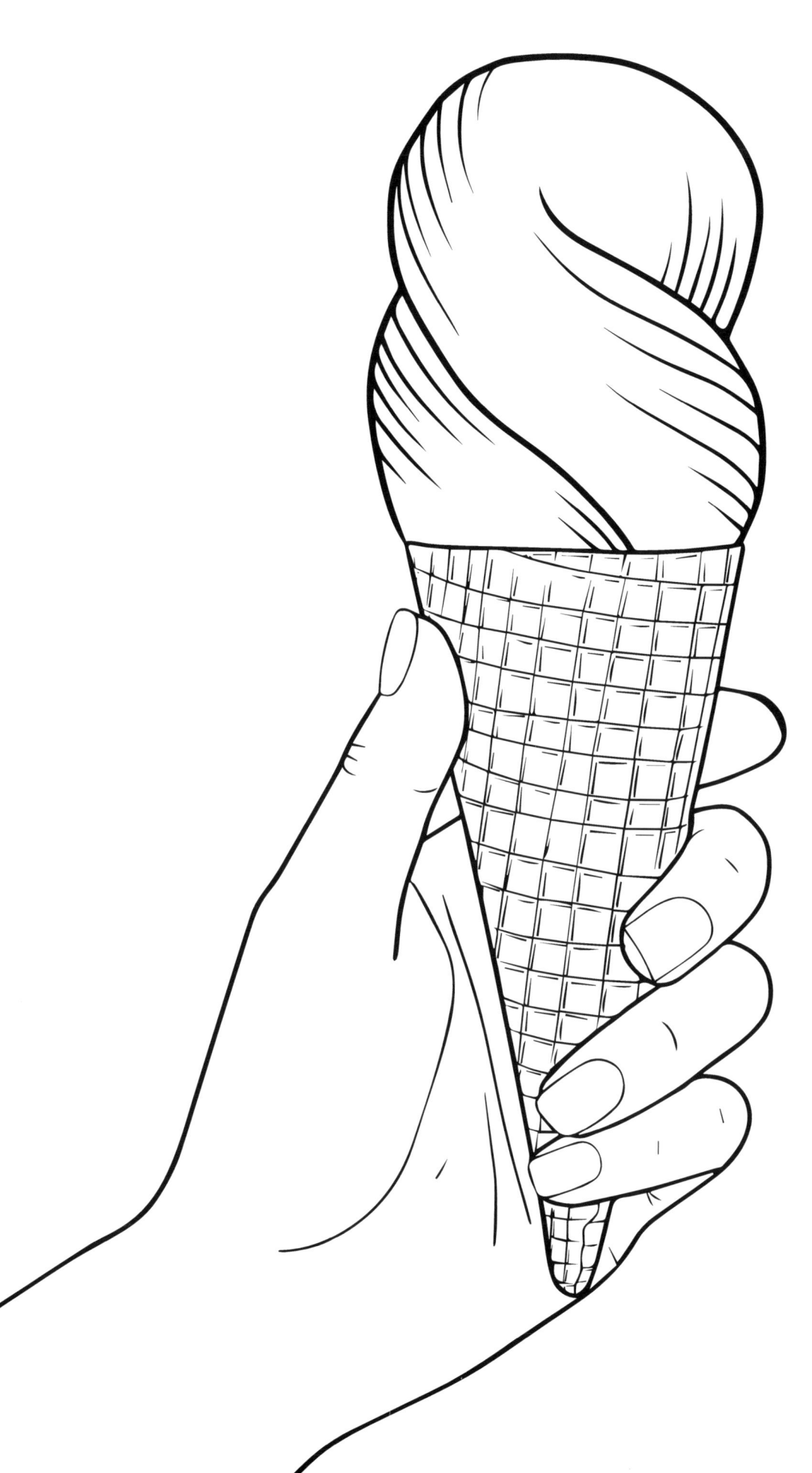

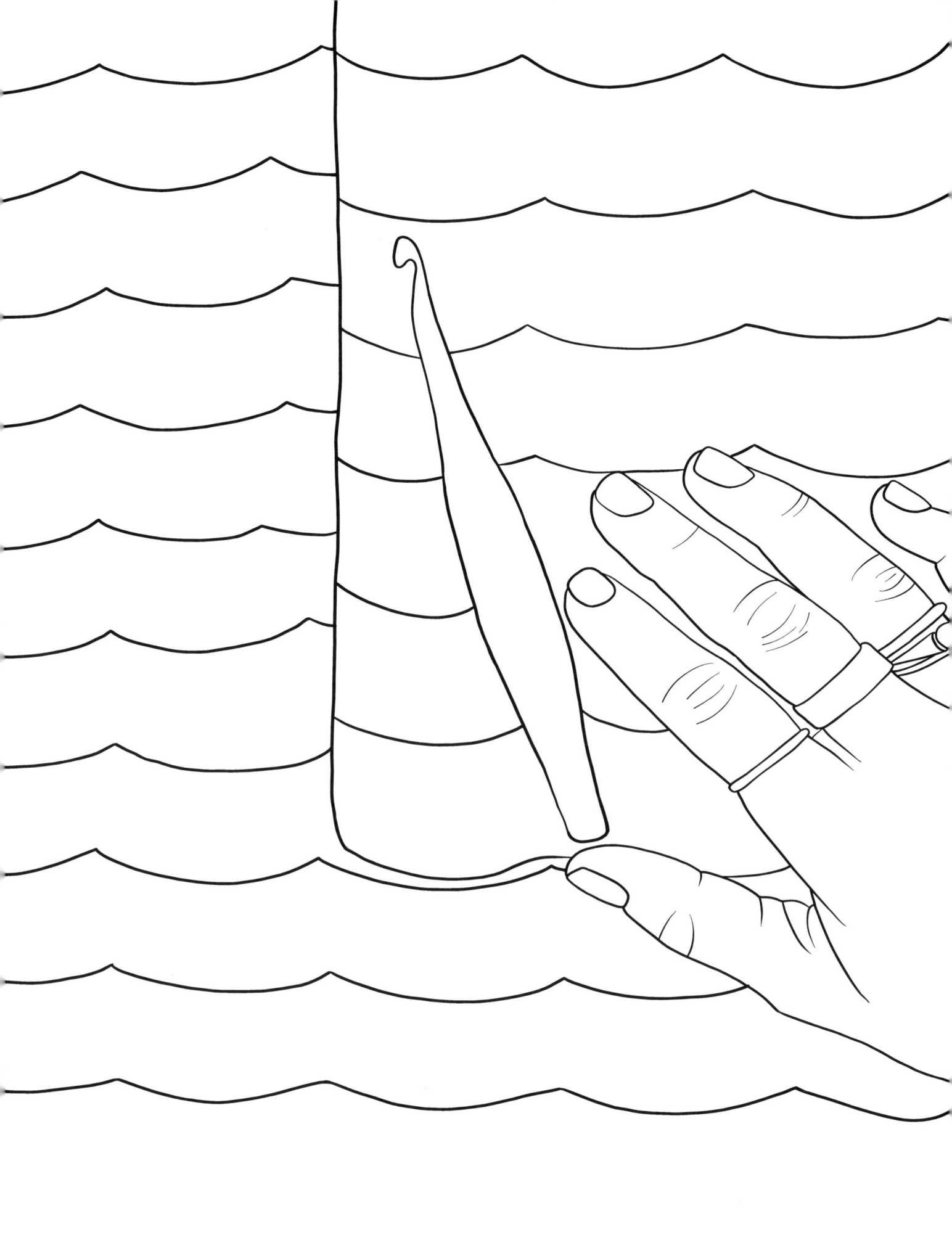